Read-About® Geography

The Four Oceans

By Wil Mara

Consultant
Nanci R. Vargus, Ed.D.
Assistant Professor of Literacy
University of Indianapolis, Indianapolis, Indiana

Children's Press®
A Division of Scholastic Inc.
New York Toronto London Auckland Sydney
Mexico City New Delhi Hong Kong
Danbury, Connecticut

Designer: Herman Adler Design
Photo Researcher: Caroline Anderson
The photos on the cover show the Pacific (top left), Indian (top right),
Atlantic (bottom right), and Arctic (bottom left) Oceans.

Library of Congress Cataloging-in-Publication Data

Mara, Wil.
  The four oceans / by Wil Mara.— 1st ed.
      p. cm. — (Rookie read-about geography)
  Includes index.
  ISBN 0-516-22749-1 (lib. bdg.)   0-516-25817-6 (pbk.)
  1. Oceanography—Juvenile literature. 2. Pacific Ocean—Juvenile
literature. 3. Arctic Ocean—Juvenile literature. 4. Atlantic Ocean—
Juvenile literature. 5. Indian Ocean—Juvenile literature. I. Title. II. Series.

  GC21.5.M35 2005
  551.46—dc22
                                      2004015573

CHILDREN'S PRESS, and ROOKIE READ-ABOUT®,
and associated logos are trademarks and or registered trademarks
of Scholastic Library Publishing. SCHOLASTIC and associated logos
are trademarks and or registered trademarks of Scholastic Inc.

1 2 3 4 5 6 7 8 9 10 R 14 13 12 11 10 09 08 07 06 05

Have you ever seen
an ocean?

This is the Pacific Ocean.

Oceans are huge. Most
of the Earth is covered
by ocean water!

There are four oceans.
They are the Pacific Ocean,
the Atlantic Ocean, the
Indian Ocean, and the
Arctic Ocean.

The Pacific Ocean is the
largest ocean. The Arctic
Ocean is the smallest ocean.

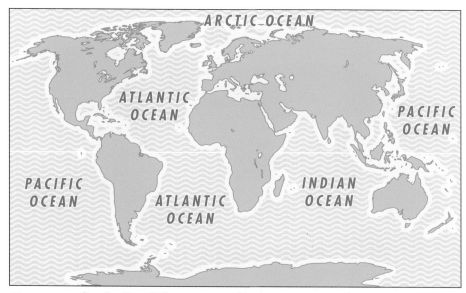

Can you find all of the oceans?

Ocean water is warmest around the middle of the Earth.

The Pacific Ocean is warm near Hawaii.

The Arctic Ocean is cold near the North Pole.

Ocean water is coldest by
the North and South Poles.

10

Many plants live in
the ocean. One kind
of plant is kelp.

Kelps live near the
top because they need
sunlight. There is no
sunlight deep in the ocean.

Many animals live in the
ocean, too.

Some animals live near the
bottom of the ocean. It is
very cold and dark there.

Some animals that live there
can light up their bodies.

Lanternfish live near the bottom of the ocean.

Some animals are very tiny. The tiniest animals are called plankton.

Some plankton can only be seen through microscopes.

Some ocean animals
are large. The blue whale
is the largest animal in
the ocean.

It is the largest animal in
the world!

Some people like to eat crabs.

Some of our food comes from the ocean. Many kinds of fish are caught there.

Lobsters, clams, and crabs come from the ocean, too. They are called shellfish.

You can swim in the
ocean. It's easy to float
in salt water.

Ships travel on the ocean, too. They carry people and things from one country to another.

The ocean can be dangerous.
In a bad storm, big waves
can damage a ship.

Many people like to
visit the ocean when the
weather is warm.

They like to eat, play, and
relax near the shore.

What do you like to do at the ocean?

These boys are building a sand castle.

Words You Know

Arctic Ocean

Atlantic Ocean

blue whale

crabs

30

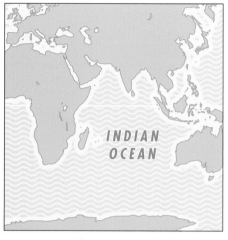

Indian Ocean

Pacific Ocean

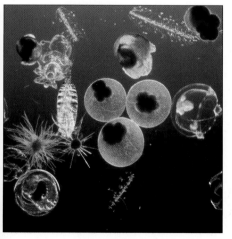

plankton

ships

31

Index

About the Author

Wil Mara is a writer who loves the ocean. He has been studying the ocean since he was a teenager. Most recently, Wil researched tidal waves for another book that he was writing.

Photo Credits